PLYMOUTH AT WAR
THROUGH TIME
Derek Tait

AMBERLEY PUBLISHING

Acknowledgements

Photograph credits : The Derek Tait Photograph Collection and Steve Johnson. Thanks to all the people who have written to me over the years sending their memories and photographs.

Thanks also to Tina Cole, Tilly Barker and Jamie Quinn.

I have tried to track down the copyright owners of all photographs used and apologise to anyone who hasn't been mentioned.

Check out my website at www.derektait.co.uk

Bibliography

Books
Images of England: Plymouth by Derek Tait (Tempus 2003).
Plymouth at War by Derek Tait (Tempus 2006).
Saltash Passage by Derek Tait (Driftwood Coast 2007).
St Budeaux by Derek Tait (Driftwood Coast 2007).
Plymouth Hoe by Derek Tait (Driftwood Coast 2008).
Memories of St Budeaux by Derek Tait (Driftwood Coast 2009).

Websites
Brian Moseley's Plymouth Data website at: www.plymouthdata.info
Derek Tait's Plymouth Local History Blog at: http://plymouthlocalhistory.blogspot.com/
Steve Johnson's Cyberheritage site at: http://www.cyber-heritage.co.uk

Newspapers
The Evening Herald   *The Western Morning News*
The Western Independent   *The Western Weekly Mercury*

First published 2011

Amberley Publishing
The Hill, Stroud
Gloucestershire, GL5 4EP

www.amberley-books.com

Copyright © Derek Tait, 2011

The right of Derek Tait to be identified as the Author of this work has been asserted in accordance with the Copyrights, Designs and Patents Act 1988.

ISBN 978 1 4456 0426 8

British Library Cataloguing in Publication Data.
A catalogue record for this book is available from the British Library.

Typeset in 9.5pt on 12pt Celeste.
Typesetting by Amberley Publishing.
Printed in the UK.

Introduction

The face of Plymouth changed completely during the Blitz of the Second World War. The narrow, bustling streets with their popular shops were obliterated and many of the city's oldest buildings were lost forever.

The heaviest attacks on Plymouth came in 1941. In the two intensive attacks on the 20th and 21st March, 336 people lost their lives. Five further attacks in April brought the toll to 590.

Hardly a building in Plymouth remained untouched by the Blitz. Much of the city centre was destroyed and although many buildings remained amongst the debris, most were damaged beyond repair.

It's hard now to imagine the total devastation the bombing caused. Many of the most popular streets, Bedford Street, Union Street, Old Town Street, Frankfort Street, Cornwall Street, George Street etc., were either totally destroyed or severely damaged. Major buildings such as the Guildhall, the Municipal Buildings, St Andrew's Church, Charles Church and the general post office were obliterated.

Many schools were also hit. These included Plymouth High School for Girls, the Hoe Grammar School and the infants' school at Summerland Place. Many churches were destroyed also including St James the Less, King Street Methodist, St Peter's, George Street Baptist and many others. The bombing was indiscriminate and destroyed anything that got in its way.

The damage to the dockyard was bad but not as damaging as would have been expected and within a few months, it was back to 90 per cent efficiency. Outside the city, the bombing was just as devastating and areas affected included Devonport, Stonehouse, St Budeaux, Swilly and Saltash Passage. Devonport lost many buildings including the post office, the Alhambra Theatre, the Synagogue, the Hippodrome and the Salvation Army Headquarters.

Residential houses that were either destroyed or beyond repair amounted to 3,754. Others that were seriously damaged but able to be repaired amounted to 18,398. Houses that were slightly damaged amounted to an additional 49,950.

It's hard to imagine today, unless you've lived through it, such devastation to a city. Children were evacuated to the countryside. Many didn't want to go and were upset that they were leaving their parents behind. Special trains were laid on and Lord and Lady Astor can be seen in photographs within this book waving them off. Older children look quite cheery to be leaving and perhaps saw the evacuation as a bit of an adventure where as many younger children were reluctant to leave.

News of the devastation of Plymouth soon reached the rest of the world and gifts arrived from all over particularly the United States who sent ambulances, soft toys, food packages and surgical dressings. The Royal Sailors Rest received crates of supplies so large that they were unable to get them into the building. Many Americans were stationed in Plymouth and they helped with clearing the debris and laid on parties for children. Some families had American servicemen staying with them. There were several camps throughout the city, including the one at Saltash Passage, in preparation for the landings on D-Day.

At the end of the war, there were a total of 4,448 casualties due to the raids and heavy bombing of the city. Throughout it all though, the people of Plymouth remained strong and there were regular dances on the Hoe almost in defiance of the enemy as they bombed the city.

Plymouth was reborn after the war and the city was rebuilt almost from scratch. Few buildings remained in the heart of the city that were there before the war and even now, the city is constantly changing. This book shows the many changes to Plymouth's centre and also shows the bomb damage to the surrounding residential areas.

Bombed out of their homes but still smiling.

Union Street

The first photograph shows Union Street busy with cars, lorries, bicycles and people. Popular shops include Burton's and H. Samuel's. The old railway arch can be seen further along the street and the Gaumont Cinema can be seen in the far distance. The cinema closed during the heavy bombing of April 1941 but reopened in May with *The Son of Monte Cristo*. The Gaumont later became the Odeon and the top of the building (now long since closed) can be seen in the later photograph.

The Far End of Union Street

The older photograph is taken from the railway arch and shows the view of Union Street looking towards the town. On the left of the earlier photograph is Hardings, a well-known name in Plymouth for many years. This part of Union Street has changed altogether although the old Gaumont/Odeon building still stands to the left of the more recent photograph.

The Odeon

The Odeon Cinema in Frankfort Street had formally been The Regent until it was sold in 1940. The first film shown at the new Odeon was *Contraband* starring Conrad Veidt. The cinema was closed during the Blitz of April 1941, but reopened two weeks later with *Men Against the Sky*.

The cinema survived the bombing and was used by Field Marshall Montgomery to brief his officers prior to D-Day. Glenn Miller gave a concert there during August 1944. After the war, New George Street replaced Frankfort Street and although the Odeon still stood, it was later demolished in 1963 and Littlewoods was built in its place.

Westwell Street

Westwell Street was badly damaged during the heavy bombing although some shops remained open and continued to trade. It ran from Bedford Street towards Princess Square. For a while Nissan huts stood in the area. It was later all pulled down and Armada Way now stands in its place. The Civic Centre dominates the scene in the later photograph.

Lockyer Street

The older view of Lockyer Street shows the Royal Hotel on the left and the Lockyer Hotel on the right. Derry's Clock can be seen in the centre of the photograph. Tramlines can be seen running along the road. At the time, all trams terminated by Derry's Clock and their destination was given as 'Theatre'. There has been much change over the years although the clock still remains in the same location.

Old Town Street

The older photograph shows Old Town Street complete with cars, buses and trams. Trams continued to run until 1945. The awning on the building on the left reads 'Maypole for Butter and Tea'. Boots the chemist is nearby. All of the old buildings have long since disappeared and what is left of Old Town Street looks nothing like it once did.

The City Centre

The older photograph shows the city as it was before the heavy bombing. St Andrew's Church can be seen towards the middle of the photograph. It's amazing that nearly every building in this picture was either severely damaged or completely destroyed. The later photograph looks from Stonehouse across the city with its many newer buildings and modern housing.

G.4856.

THE BATHING POOL, PLYMOUTH.

The Lido

The one-time popular Lido was officially opened in 1935. During the war, people flocked to the pool to bathe after spending the day clearing up rubble. During one night alone, over 3,000 tickets were sold. At other times, orchestras played on the terraces while swimmers swam nearby and regular beauty contests were held around the pool. It seemed to lose its appeal in later years but has now been refurbished although it isn't as popular as it once was.

Derry's Clock

Derry's Clock can be seen amongst the bomb damage to the city in the older photograph. The clock and the bank to its right still survive but everything else has disappeared. The Theatre Royal now stands on the left in the later photograph and in the background is the imposing Civic Centre building which was opened in 1962.

Old Town Street Destruction

The older photograph shows the total devastation caused to Old Town Street by the enemy bombing. Men from the Home Guard help to clear away the rubble and debris. Today, the area is busy with shoppers and people relaxing outside one of the many nearby cafés. In the distance of the newer photograph, the Drake Circus Mall can just be seen in the background.

The Prysten House

The Prysten House was built in the fifteenth century as a dwelling for the priest who served the nearby St Andrew's Church. It was affected by the heavy bombing of 1941 and the earlier photograph shows some of the damage. Over the years, it has been used for many things. At the end of the nineteenth century, it was a grocer's and today, it's home to the TV chefs, the Tanner Brothers, who run a successful restaurant from there.

The Post Office

The post office stood in Westwell Street opposite Guildhall Square. It was opened in 1884 and built of Portland Stone at a cost of £16,500. Its interior was reconstructed in 1933 and it featured an inlaid floor depicting Sir Francis Drake's ship *The Mayflower*. Badly damaged, it moved to new premises at Spears Corner in Tavistock Road and after the war, moved to Old Town Street. Westwell Street has long since been demolished and the wide sweep of Armada Way takes its place.

Millbay Station

Railway stations were a strategic target for enemy bombing. The older photograph shows two bomb craters nearby. Ironically, one of the posters on the wall on the right says, 'Welcome to Plymouth'. Naval personnel can be seen in the background helping to remove the debris. On the left of the photograph is the Duke of Cornwall Hotel. Today, the Pavilions stand where the station once stood.

St Andrew's Church

On 20 March 1941, St Andrew's Church was severely damaged during a bombing raid and later suffered from a further attack. After the bombing, a headmistress placed a wooden sign over the North door with the word, 'Resurgam' meaning 'I will rise again'. The word is now carved in stone above the main door. For a while, St Andrew's operated as a 'garden church' and services continued to be held there. It wasn't until 1957 that the church was repaired and re-consecrated.

The Athenaeum

The Athenaeum was designed by John Foulston and the foundation stone was laid in 1818. It was badly damaged during the war but wasn't demolished until November 1959. The building that stands in its place today was opened in 1961. As well as a 340 seat theatre, it includes a library, a lecture room and lounge.

Drake Circus

In the older photograph, the Guinness Clock and the words 'Guinness is good for you' can be seen on the building belonging to the Liverpool Victoria Friendly Society. The clock was put in place in April 1937 and along with the sign, was illuminated. By the time demolition of Drake Circus began in 1960, it was rusted and the tubes which illuminated it had been destroyed mainly by the bombing during the Blitz. It was carefully taken down and stored away but eventually there was a clear out and the whole thing, unfortunately, ended up at the rubbish tip at Chelson Meadow.

The Guildhall

In the older photograph, Winston Churchill can be seen visiting the city on 2 May 1941 after the devastating bombing of the city. Behind him can be seen the Guildhall Tower. Churchill was visibly upset and he told the people, 'Your homes are down but your hearts are high!' His visit boosted morale but the people of Plymouth still had to endure another four years of war.

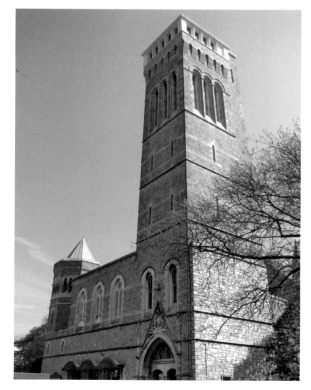

Frankfort Street

The older photograph was taken from the offices of the *Western Morning News* building and shows fireman dousing down the smouldering premises nearby. The store belonging to Cohens can be seen further up the street. The later photograph shows the more modern buildings of New George Street that replaced the demolished Frankfort Street. The empty Woolworths store stands on the right.

Costers in Frankfort Street

The earlier photograph shows Costers in Frankfort Street on fire just before the roof collapsed. Amazingly, the *Western Morning News* building to its right survived the bombing. Today, the Santander building occupies the area where Costers once stood. Coincidently, Waterstone's, next door, serves Costa Coffee although, of course, there is no connection.

Frankfort Street

The older photograph shows the many damaged buildings in Frankfort Street. Shops belonging to Wride's and V. B. Mills can be seen in the picture and workers are nearby clearing away the rubble. Today, Frankfort Street is New George Street and the shops opposite Waterstone's replace the buildings in the earlier photograph. This part of the town isn't as busy as it once was since the mall at Drake Circus was built.

Bank of England Place

The older photograph shows the area as viewed from the Royal Cinema. The illuminated sign marks the spot where the underground toilets once stood near to Derry's Clock. The later photograph shows two survivors of the Blitz – Derry's Clock and the bank which is now The Bank Public House. The council offices of the Civic Centre can be seen in the background.

The *Western Morning News* Building

The earlier photograph shows the *Western Morning News* building being hosed down to stop fires spreading from other buildings. Today, the building is one of the few survivors in the main part of Plymouth. It houses the bookstore, Waterstone's. All the buildings surrounding it today were built after the war. The Odeon opposite also survived but today is long gone and the area is occupied by T. J. Hughes.

Drake Circus

Much bomb damage can be seen in the area known as Drake Circus. On the right of the older photograph can be seen the building belonging to the Liverpool Victoria Friendly Society. The area has changed vastly over the years. In 1968, many buildings were demolished for a more modern shopping centre to be built. This was completed and opened in 1971. In 2004, a new shopping centre was built – the Mall. It's loved by some but loathed by others.

Charles Church

The older photograph shows American servicemen, complete with an anti-aircraft gun, in the centre of Plymouth. The devastation to the area is clear to see. Charles Church can be seen in the background. The later photograph shows the area today looking from Bretonside. On the left can be seen the new Drake Shopping Mall and Charles Church can be seen on the right. The bus station is in the foreground.

Old Town Street

Fred Notcutt's photography studio can be seen on the left of the earlier photograph. It specialised in Naval and Military photography. The Guinness clock can be seen in the background and much destruction has been caused to nearby buildings. The area today is home to banks and also to the main post office. In the background is the Drake Shopping Mall.

The Pier

The Pier is shown here completely burnt out after being bombed in 1941. In the background can be seen Drake's Island. The remains of the Pier were removed in 1953 and today, it's hard to tell that it was ever there. The wall, which doubles as a seating area in the later photograph, marks the spot where the entrance to the Pier once was.

Bomb Disposal

The older photograph shows men of the bomb disposal team removing an unexploded bomb. Many bombs fell on Plymouth and many failed to go off. Recently, in Notte Street where the old NAAFI building once stood, two unexploded bombs were discovered while the building was being demolished. The area was cordoned off and the bombs were made safe by the MOD Explosive Ordnance Disposal team before being removed and destroyed off Cawsand Bay.

The Hoe Foreshore

The foreshore and buildings are shown damaged in the early photograph. Deckchairs can be seen piled against a nearby wall. In the background is Smeaton's Tower which was painted all in one colour at the time. Today, it's painted in its original colour scheme, red and white. The popular Terrace Café now occupies the damaged building shown in the first photograph although most of the area remains much the same.

The Belvedere

The older photograph shows damage near to the Belvedere. At this point, the houses in the distance still remained intact although they were later destroyed and demolished. For many years the area in the background was an empty bomb site but in recent years, the very modern Azure apartment building has been built in its place. The area in the foreground all looks very similar today.

Drake's Statue

The older photograph shows a barrage balloon close to Sir Francis Drake's statue on the Hoe. The statue was unveiled by Lady Elliot Drake, a descendant of Drake, in front of 20,000 people on 14 February 1884. The day was observed in the three towns as a holiday. The later photograph shows his statue together with the war memorial and the very popular Big Wheel.

Elliot Terrace

The earlier photograph shows Winston Churchill and his wife visiting the Astors at their home in Elliot Terrace. The Astors entertained many celebrities there including Charlie Chaplin, Amy Johnson, George Bernard Shaw and Noel Coward. The later photograph shows a skateboarder passing by the terrace as he skates along the Promenade on the Hoe. On the left is the Grand Hotel where Laurel and Hardy once stayed.

The Bandstand

The bandstand was removed so that its metal could be used to help the war effort. The earlier photograph shows members of a barrage balloon team salvaging what they can. The bandstand was to the left of Smeaton's Tower in the later photograph. It was never rebuilt but it's possible to see where it once stood from the indentations in the grass.

Damaged Pier

The earlier photograph shows the destroyed entrance to the Pier. The circular piece of concrete is part of the housing of the Pier's once ornate clock. Not much is left and it's hard to imagine it as the busy meeting place that it once was. Today, people sit in the same spot looking out to the Sound eating ice-creams from the nearby stall or just enjoying the excellent view.

Dancing on the Hoe

Children can be seen dancing on the Hoe in the older photograph. During the war years, dancing brought many people together and some people travelled miles to take part. It helped take their minds off the devastation to the city. In the background can be seen Drake's Island and to the right, Mount Edgcumbe. Occasionally, dances still take place on the Hoe Promenade in the summer months.

Concert on the Hoe

The older photograph shows a young girl singing on the Hoe accompanied by a military band. One of the soldiers has a guitar and the corporal in the picture is playing a clarinet. I wonder what the song was? Much of the Hoe has remained the same over the years although some dwellings and the bandstand are now long gone.

GI's Dancing on the Hoe Promenade
The older photograph shows
American Army personnel dancing on
the Hoe Promenade. Smeaton's Tower
can be seen in the background. This
picture would have probably been
taken during 1943, or soon after, when
there was a big American presence in
the city in the run up to D-Day. The
only Americans on the Hoe nowadays
are tourists. The later photograph
shows many people enjoying the fine
weather by the lighthouse.

Nancy Astor Dancing on the Hoe
Lady Astor can be seen in the older photograph dancing with a soldier on the Hoe. Noel Coward said at the time, 'After all that devastation, on a summer evening, people were dancing on the Hoe. It made me cry – the bravery, the gallantry, the Englishness of it!' Sir Francis Drake's statue can be seen in the background.

Digging for Victory

The Home Guard can be seen in the older photograph taking part in the Digging for Victory campaign on Plymouth Hoe. A dog is also helping out in the photograph as two sailors watch on. With food shortages, many of Plymouth's city parks were turned into allotments. Here, the crop is potatoes. Vegetables were not rationed but were often in short supply. People who had gardens were encouraged to plant vegetables instead of flowers.

Lockyer Street

Lockyer Street can be seen badly damaged in the older photograph. A sign on the wall reads, 'To the ARP Shelter'. A policeman and several other people can be seen gathered nearby. The newer photograph shows the far end of Lockyer Street heading down towards the multi-storey car park and Derry's Clock. The Bank Public House is in the distance on the right of the picture.

Leigham Street

Leigham Street, close to the Hoe, can be seen badly damaged in the older photograph. One house has taken a direct hit. Today, Leigham Street is still there and joins Citadel Road, which can be seen in the background. Today, most of Leigham Street is taken up by the Azure complex. Plymouth Marine Laboratory stands on the ground opposite and there is also a small car park.

Mulgrave Street

Mulgrave Street can be found back from Notte Street. It was heavily damaged during the bombing and it's hard to match anything of the street today to how it once was pre-war. The later photograph shows Lockyer Street in the background and the tall building is Phoenix House. For many years there has been a residential care home in Mulgrave Street.

Athenaeum Terrace

The older photograph shows Athenaeum Terrace as taken from the ground in front of the Crescent. A bomb has totally destroyed a large section in this row of office buildings. The Terrace was designed by George Wightwick who worked with John Foulston. Nearby, the Westward Television Studios were later built but the building has now been demolished and is under development.

Notte Street

The buildings on the left of the older picture have been totally destroyed and the debris from them covers the pavement. The later photograph shows a complete rebuilding of Notte Street although some older buildings still remain further towards the Barbican. On the right of the newer photograph is the Barclays Bank building which now forms apartments at Berkeley Square.

The Continental Hotel

On a February night in 1943, a bomb exploded on the road in front of the Continental Hotel. It was a Saturday and 300 people were inside dancing. Every window was blown out of the hotel but luckily, no-one was injured. Today, along with the Duke of Cornwall Hotel nearby, it gives an idea of the grandeur of hotels that once served the very busy railway close by at Millbay Station.

Damage at Millbay Station

Rubble lies beside and on the railway line at Millbay Station in the earlier photograph. The Duke of Cornwall Hotel can be seen in the background. The station is long gone and, as mentioned earlier, the Pavilions now stand in its place. The later photograph shows the remaining posts that marked the entrance to the station.

Sutton Harbour

The older photograph shows the extent of the bomb damage to Sutton Harbour with wrecked buildings and a sunken boat. The area today is very busy with tourists exploring the Barbican and the nearby cobbled streets. Fishing boats mingle with the many expensive private yachts that are moored there. In the background, modern, tall buildings dominate the skyline, which includes offices and apartments.

The Octagon

In the earlier photograph, buildings can be seen collapsing due to fire caused by a bombing raid. The later photograph shows the view taken from the Octagon along Union Street towards the Palace Theatre. It's easy to see that many of the old buildings in the area have been lost over the years and have been replaced with more modern flats.

The Far End of Union Street

A policeman surveys the damage at the far end of Union Street in the older photograph. On the right is the '30 shillings tailor' whose slogan was 'Weaver to Wearer'. A huge advert for Capstan cigarettes can be seen in the background. Much has been cleared away over the years and newer buildings have included car showrooms as well as Aldi and Lidl supermarkets.

Approaching Stonehouse Bridge
In the earlier photograph, Stonehouse Bridge can be seen on the left. Severe damage has been caused to the nearby shops. The building in the background belonged to Frederick Strang who repaired boots. Next door to him was J. Bremner who ran a general store. The later photograph shows the roundabout at the end of Union Street, approaching Stonehouse Bridge and looking towards Brickfields.

Union Street

Much of Union Street is seen on fire in the earlier photograph and many of the older buildings were completely destroyed. Some of the original buildings still exist in the area, like the Palace Theatre, but most are neglected and some are left to fall into ruin. The Palace Theatre is a beautiful building but has been in a poor state for many years now.

Stonehouse Town Hall

The Town Hall in Stonehouse stood at the end of Emma Place. A plaque marks the spot where it once was. It was erected between 1849 and 1850 and was Italian in style. It was designed by Fuller & Gingell of Bristol. Today, the area is occupied by garages and industrial units although the buildings on the right remain intact.

Fore Street, Devonport

The older photograph shows the bomb damaged buildings of Fore Street. The shop belonging to David Greig can be seen on the left and the Forum Cinema can be seen further up the street. Today, only the Forum Cinema (now Mecca Bingo) building survives and the street has totally altered. Post war flats can be seen in the background.

The Forum, Fore Street

The earlier photograph shows the Forum Cinema and Fore Street from the other direction. The street is badly damaged and a man wearing a military helmet can be seen. For many years, the far end of Fore Street fell within the confines of the dockyard but it has recently been opened up and new housing has been built.

Steam Rollers at Fore Street

The older photograph shows much of Fore Street in ruins after heavy bombing. Two steam rollers are compressing the ground so that traffic can move through freely. It would be hard to recognise the area today from this photograph. The newer photograph shows the recently built housing and two cyclists can be seen heading in the direction of the Forum.

Destruction of Fore Street

Before the bombing, Fore Street was a bustling area with shops that included Woolworths, Timothy Whites, British Home Stores, Tozers, Boots, Liptons and Marks & Spencers. There were three cinemas including the Tivoli, the Electric and the Forum. The scene today has changed completely and the later photograph shows the street as it is opposite the Forum. The buildings on the left include the Devonport Playhouse.

Devonport Railway Station

The older photograph shows the line through Devonport strewn with rubble and debris. The building's windows have been boarded up and the line has been put out of action. The station at Kings Road, Devonport, was closed to passengers in 1964 and the College of Further Education was built on the site. Today, it has been renamed City College Plymouth.

Royal William Victualling Yard

The older photograph was taken on 30 March 1944 and shows US Harbour Craft Vessels. The Royal William Victualling Yard can be seen in the background. The Americans were in the area prior to the D-Day landings at Normandy. The later photograph shows the area today. The Royal William Yard now consists of luxury apartments and studios and there are many expensive yachts moored nearby.

Richmond Wharf
In the older photograph, a US Army tugboat can be seen moored up at Richmond Wharf during March 1944. These were used to move larger vessels in and out of port. Today, Richmond Wharf is the home of luxury yachts as well as smaller boats. The apartments have been built to cater for their owners. In the background can be seen Mount Wise.

Barton Avenue, Ford

Barton Avenue is shown in a poor state in the earlier photograph with rubble and debris covering the street. A woman on the left of the picture sits on the pavement with a few rescued possessions. People look at the desolation in disbelief, as one man tries to push his bicycle through the bricks and twisted masonry that covers the road.

Furneaux Avenue, Swilly

It's hard to imagine that this was once all that was left of Furneaux Avenue after the heavy bombing of the area. End walls of houses miraculously stay standing on their own. The homes were later rebuilt and the area was renamed North Prospect. Today, North Prospect is being regenerated with over 1,200 new homes being built and 360 homes being refurbished.

Greenbank Hospital

Opened in 1840, Greenbank Hospital served the people of Plymouth until it was closed in the 1990s. The hospital was bombed during the night of Monday, 13 January 1941. The older photograph shows one of the badly damaged wards. Luckily, no-one was killed although two nurses were injured. A small housing estate stands on the area today but the gateposts that were once at the entrance of the hospital still stand.

St Augustine's Church

St Augustine's Church stood beside Alexandra Road where it meets Ashford Hill in Lipson. The older photograph shows many onlookers watching as men work to clear the debris. Although badly damaged, the church was later rebuilt and reopened in 1954. The church was completely demolished several years ago and today, a new housing development called Chapel 24 is waiting to be built in its place.

Sungates, Hartley

Sungates has been an iconic Plymouth landmark for many years. It was built in 1934 and is thought to be a copy of Errol Flynn's Hollywood home. The older photograph shows it badly damaged and a burnt out motor car lies nearby. It was later rebuilt and today it looks much the same as it did before the bombing.

Plymouth Argyle

When the stand was bombed, not only did Plymouth lose part of its football ground but also many Plymothians lost their furniture which was kept at the ground for safe keeping. It was felt that the ground was far enough away from the centre of Plymouth to avoid the bombs. The ground was reopened at the end of the war in time for the resumption of the football league in 1945.

Verna Road, St Budeaux

St Budeaux was hit several times by bombs probably intended for the nearby dockyard and the Royal Albert Bridge. Besides Verna Road, other places hit in St Budeaux included the railway station, an armaments barge at Saltash Passage and dwellings along Victoria Road and Wolseley Road. Some houses have been rebuilt but in other areas, large spaces still remain.

Lord Astor and an Evacuee, North Road Station

Lord Astor can be seen in the older photograph shaking the hand of a little boy who is about to be evacuated. The boy has with him his suitcase and his gas mask. He also has a parcel label fixed to him with his name and address in case he gets lost on the journey. He looks quite happy but probably wasn't!

Lady Astor and Evacuees, North Road Station

Many children were evacuated to the countryside to stay with relatives and family friends. The city was seen as too dangerous for children especially after the Blitz of 1941. Many saw it as an adventure but many were very upset to be leaving their parents behind. The station is still in the same place today and the later photograph also shows the large office building nearby.

The Queen's Messengers, Central Park

The Queen's Messengers Convoy were a familiar sight in and around Plymouth. They were set up to feed the homeless and supply warm food and drink to people without electric and water supplies. The Queen's Messenger Food Convoys were named after Queen Elizabeth (the mother of today's Queen Elizabeth) who donated money for the first eighteen convoys. The earlier photograph was taken where the park and ride car park is today at Central Park.

St Budeaux Station

The first photograph shows the Queen's Messengers Convoy dishing out soup and tea to local people and servicemen at St Budeaux station. The poster on the left advertises Devonport's Electric Cinema which is showing 'Strike Up the Band' starring Mickey Rooney and Judy Garland. The same area today is just a busy road and a crossing leading to the local Co-op. It's hard to imagine that all this wartime activity once took place there.

D-Day, Saltash Passage

The above photograph shows the smiling faces of some of the American servicemen on the morning they boarded their ships at Saltash Passage to head off for D-Day. Unfortunately, many didn't survive. The tranquil scene today is devoid of naval vessels but features many yachts, dinghies and other pleasure boats. Brunel's Royal Albert Bridge can be seen in the background of the later photograph.

Vicarage Road Camp, St Budeaux

The older photograph shows Vicarage Road Camp in St Budeaux together with some of the American survivors of the unfortunate Slapton Sands exercise in April 1944. They were later sent to Exeter for new uniforms before being re-assigned to different units and sent to Europe for D-Day. Today, the area is grassed and features a small car park overlooking the Brunel and Tamar Bridges.

St Budeaux Station after the Bombing

The station was popular with sailors, dockyard workers and tourists travelling to and from work and also to Cornwall over the Royal Albert Bridge. It became a target for the Luftwaffe who were not only trying to disrupt transport but were also trying to hit the nearby dockyard as well as the bridge and armaments depot at Ernesettle. The station is still open today but all that remains beside the line is a small shelter.

Millbay Docks

This older photograph shows the captured German Submarine U-1023 at Millbay Docks. The captain appears to be in the photograph on the left. In the background can be seen the old grain silo which was built in 1940. It was felt to be a landmark for enemy bombers so Lord Astor suggested that it be painted in camouflage colours. It remained in place until it was demolished in 2009.

Prince Rock

The earlier photograph was taken by an American serviceman stationed in Plymouth. On the left is a double-decker bus advertising 'Modern Woman' and 'E. Dingle & Co' on the back. In the distance can be seen Prince Rock on the left and what is now the road to Plymstock on the right. The houses on the left still survive but the ones in the centre of the older photograph are long gone. The area today is plagued by road works.

St Peter's Chapel, Saltash Passage

The chapel was built in 1885 and once stood in Saltash Passage. It was damaged by enemy bombing in April 1941 and was removed in the 1950s. The area today is used as a storage space for Donne's boatyard. The later photograph shows the view in the other direction across the Tamar looking towards Coombe Viaduct and Cornwall.

Westwell Street and the Guildhall Tower

The older photograph shows the damage to Westwell Street looking towards the Guildhall. Military vehicles have blocked off the road as local people stand and watch. R. Humm and Co. can be seen on the left and the Norwich Union Building stands on the right. Today, all of this area has been cleared and is almost unrecognisable apart from the tower which dominates the scene.

Frankfort Street

Frankfort Street later became New George Street after the rebuilding of the city. Many of the buildings seen in the earlier photograph were later demolished and cleared away. The *Western Morning News* building on the right survived the Blitz but many of the other buildings in the area were totally destroyed. Today, the *Western Morning News* building houses one of my favourite Plymouth shops, Waterstone's.

Tin Pan Alley

Tin Pan Alley became the temporary home of the market stall holders who had once occupied the Pannier Market. The space within the market was given over to major stores like Marks & Spencers and Woolworths so that they could continue trading. Tin Pan Alley was located at the top of Cornwall Street which, at the time, was Drake Street.

Tavistock Road / North Hill

American troops can be seen marching down Tavistock Road (later North Hill). Many people have turned out to see them including young children who were fascinated by US soldiers. In the background can be seen Sherwell United Reformed Church. Underneath their feet can be seen the old tram lines. Easily recognisable today, the area is very busy with traffic and students from the nearby university.

Marching by the Museum

In the earlier photograph, members of the Land Army march by the city museum. By 1940, agriculture had lost 30,000 men to the British Army and another 15,000 to other vital work. The severe shortage of labour prompted the government to form the Land Army. By 1944, there were over 80,000 women working on the land doing anything from milking and general farm work to cutting down trees and working in saw mills. The later photograph shows the same area today.

A Band Marches by the Guildhall

The earlier photograph shows an American jazz band passing close to the damaged Guildhall. They were marking the occasion of 'Salute the Soldier Week' in 1944. City dignitaries including Lord and Lady Astor can be seen watching the event. Today, the Guildhall has been rebuilt and all of the buildings seen in the old photograph have gone forever.

VE Day, Guildhall Square

The older photograph shows the VE Day celebrations in Guildhall Square. A large crowd has gathered around the Guildhall to listen to dignitaries and members of the armed forces. The church bells rang out over the city; previously they had been banned except to announce an enemy invasion. The later photograph looks towards the Guildhall from Royal Parade.

VE Day Celebrations, Saltburn Road, St Budeaux

On a smaller scale, the older photograph shows VE Day celebrations in Saltburn Road in St Budeaux. There are long tables set up and children are happily enjoying the party laid on by their mothers and other members of the community. There are many old fashioned prams and one push chair looks very home-made. The later photograph shows the same area today.

The Top of Royal Parade

In the earlier photograph, the main roads of Royal Parade are in place and being used by traffic including cars and double-decker buses. Trams have become a thing of the past. The buildings, which would later become the city's major stores, are still under construction. At the time, it would all be seen to be very modern.

King George VI and Queen Elizabeth

The King and Queen unveil an inscription commemorating the rebuilding of the city in 1947. The Prudential Building dominates the scene and the balconies on the building hold many spectators. Thousands of people have gathered to watch. The couple later visited the Astors at their home in Elliot Terrace on the Hoe. The later photograph shows the same stretch, now Armada Way.

Royal Parade

This photograph shows the new Royal Parade being built sometime around 1947. In this picture, several buildings have survived the bombing including the Co-op on the left, the Odeon Cinema behind it and the *Western Morning News* building on the right. Today, the area is dominated by the newer buildings built in the late 1940s and 1950s.

Armada Way

Barclays Bank was one of the first buildings to be erected in Armada Way after the war. Temporary Nissen huts can be seen in the centre of the older photograph as well as many of the older buildings that survived the bombing. The later photograph shows the same area today as it heads up towards Smeaton's Tower and Plymouth Hoe.

The Building of Royal Parade

The older photograph shows the new roads of Royal Parade in about 1947. By this time, they were already well used by buses, vans and cars although a lot of the new city still had to be rebuilt. On the right of the photograph can be seen the newly built Armada Way. The later photograph shows Royal Parade as it is today complete with a constant flow of traffic.

New Buildings, Royal Parade

The older photograph shows the construction of new stores beside Royal Parade. Many of the older buildings seen in this photograph would later be demolished to make way for the new development. The later photograph shows Royal Parade as seen from Derry's Cross roundabout. Pearl Assurance House can be seen in the background as well as the now vacated Co-op building.

Charles Church and Exeter Street

Charles Church, although severely damaged, remains standing today as a monument to Plymouth's war dead. The older photograph shows the newly built roads nearby. For many years, a multi-storey car park stood behind the church. Today, this has been demolished and replaced by the weird and wonderful Drake Circus Shopping Mall. It's certainly an odd building but is easily located by tourists.

The Bottom of Royal Parade
The earlier photograph shows the lower end of Royal Parade being constructed. In the distance can be seen the Guildhall, St Andrew's Church and also the spire of the destroyed Charles Church. Slowly, the remaining buildings were cleared away to make way for a more modern, spacious shopping centre. The later photograph shows a much leafier, greener area.

Raleigh Street

The area is under redevelopment in the earlier photograph and the Odeon in Frankfort Street (later New George Street) can be seen on the right. Although there are buildings in the photograph that survived the war, all were later cleared away to make way for the new development. Raleigh Street became a well used shopping area at the bottom of town but with many recent store closures, it's perhaps not as popular as it once was.